My Friends and I

Longman

CHAPTER

5

We Have Fun Together

How do we have fun?

We are sliding.

It's fun.

We are playing ball.
It's fun.

I am swinging.
It's fun.

What is fun for you to do?

What do friends do together?

Friends play.

Friends draw.

Friends help each other.

What other things do friends do?

Our faces show how we feel.

I feel happy.

I feel sad.

I feel angry.

I feel glad.

How do you look when you're sad?
How do you look when you're happy?

Body Shapes

Point to a group of children.

What shape do they make?

Try it!

Tell what you learned.

1. Point to the children who are swinging.

2. Point to a happy child. How do you know the child is happy?

3. What do you do with a friend? Draw a picture.

CHAPTER 6

Our Bodies

What can we do?

I can swing!
I have strong arms.

I can jump!
I have strong legs.

I can zip!

I can ride!

What can you do with your hands and arms?

What can you do with your feet and legs?

We are healthy!

I eat good food.

I brush my teeth.

I play outside.

I sleep.

How do you stay healthy?

Are they the same?
Are they different?

They are different.
I can feel it.

They are different.
I can hear it.

They are different.

We can see it.

They are the same.

I can smell it!

I can taste it!

What do you use to tell if something is the same or different?

What's in the Bag?

Put some things in a bag.

Ask a friend to touch one thing and guess what it is.

Tell what you learned.

1. What is the girl doing? Show me.

2. Touch the shapes.
Are they the same?

How do you know?

3. Draw a picture of yourself doing
something healthy.

My Toys

We like to play.

What do you see?

I am playing
a game.

I am building.

Which toy do you like?

Where is it?

What do you see?

I have a car.

It is on the shelf.

I have a ball.

It is under the bed.

Where do you put your toys?

Let's play!

I want a ball.

I want a yellow ball.

I am buying this one.

What do you want to buy?

Game Time

Cleanup!

Touch a toy. Say its name.

How many do you see?

Count them.

Tell what you learned.

1. Touch the toy on the bed.
   Say its name.

2. Touch the toy under the bed.
   Say its name.

3. Draw a toy that you like.
   What color is it?